# Praying with Jesus

by
Pope Benedict XVI

*All booklets are published thanks to the
generous support of the members of the
Catholic Truth Society*

CATHOLIC TRUTH SOCIETY
PUBLISHERS TO THE HOLY SEE

# Contents

*All rights reserved. First published 2013 by The Incorporated Catholic Truth Society, 40-46 Harleyford Road London SE11 5AY Tel: 020 7640 0042 Fax: 020 7640 0046. © Libreria Editrice Vaticana. This edition © The Incorporated Catholic Truth Society 2013.*

*ISBN 978 1 86082 844 7*

# Prayer Throughout the Life of Jesus

In our previous Catecheses we have reflected on several examples of prayer in the Old Testament. Today I would like to begin to look at Jesus, at his prayer that flows through the whole of his life like a secret channel that waters existence, relationships and actions, and guides them, with progressive firmness, to the total gift of self in accordance with the loving plan of God the Father. Jesus is also our Teacher in prayer, indeed he is our active and fraternal support on every occasion that we address the Father. Truly, "prayer", as it is summed up in a heading in the *Compendium of the Catechism of the Catholic Church,* "is fully revealed and realised in Jesus" (nn. 541-547). Let us also look at him in our forthcoming Catecheses.

## Prayer after baptism

The prayer that followed the baptism in the River Jordan to which he submitted is an especially important moment on his journey. The Evangelist Luke notes that Jesus - after having received baptism at the hands of John the Baptist together with all the people - enters into an intensely personal and prolonged prayer: "When all the people were baptised, and when Jesus also had been baptised and was praying, the heaven was opened, and the Holy Spirit descended upon him" (*Lk* 3:21-22). The fact that he "was praying", in conversation with the Father, illuminated the act he had carried out along with so many of his people who had flocked to the banks of the Jordan. By praying, he gave his action, baptism, an exclusively personal character.

## Baptism means change

The Baptist had launched a forceful appeal to live truly as "children to Abraham", being converted to goodness and bearing fruit worthy of this change (cf. *Lk* 3:7-9). And a large number of Israelites had felt impelled to act, as Mark the Evangelist recalled, writing: "There went out to him [to John] all the country of Judea, and all the people of Jerusalem; and they were baptised by him in the River Jordan, confessing their sins" (*Mk* 1:5). The Baptist was bringing something really new: to undergo baptism was to mark a decisive turning point, leaving behind forms of conduct linked to sin and starting a new life. Jesus too accepted this invitation; he joined the grey multitude of sinners waiting on the banks of the Jordan.

## Jesus is one with sinners

However, a question also wells up in us, as it did in the early Christians: why did Jesus voluntarily submit to this baptism of penance and conversion? He had no sins to confess, he had not sinned, hence he was in no need of conversion. So what accounts for his action? The Evangelist Matthew records the amazement of the Baptist who stated: "I need to be baptised by you, and do you come to me?" (*Mt* 3:14), and Jesus' response: "Let it be so now; for thus it is fitting for us to fulfil all righteousness" (v. 15). The word "righteousness" in the biblical world means the acceptance of God's will without reserve. Jesus showed his closeness to that part of his people who, following the Baptist, recognised that it was not enough merely to consider themselves children of Abraham, and wanted to do God's will, wanted to commit themselves to ensuring that their behaviour was a faithful response to the Covenant God had offered through Abraham. Therefore by entering the River Jordan, Jesus, without sin, showed his solidarity with those who recognise their sins, who choose to repent and to change their lives; Jesus made it clear that being part of the People of God means entering into a perspective of newness of life, of life in accordance with God.

## Jesus' bond with the Father

In this action Jesus anticipated the Cross; he began his ministry by taking his place among sinners, by taking upon his shoulders the burden of the whole of humanity and by doing the Father's will. Recollected in prayer, Jesus showed his profound bond with the Father who is in Heaven, he experienced his fatherhood, understood the demanding beauty of his love and, in conversation with the Father, received the confirmation of his mission. The words that resounded from Heaven (cf. *Lk* 3:22), anticipated a reference to the Paschal Mystery, the Cross and the Resurrection. The divine voice called him "my beloved Son", recalling Isaac, the beloved son whom Abraham, his father, was prepared to sacrifice, in accordance with God's command (cf. *Gn* 22:1-14). Jesus was not only *the son of David*, of royal, messianic lineage, or *the Servant* with whom God was well pleased; he was also the *only begotten Son*, beloved, like Isaac, whom God the Father gave for the world's salvation. At the moment when, through prayer, Jesus was experiencing the depth of his own sonship and God's fatherhood (cf. *Lk* 3:22b), the Holy Spirit, whom he was to pour out after being raised on the Cross (cf. *Jn* 1:32-34; 7:37-39), descended upon him (cf. *Lk* 3:22a) and guided him in his mission that he might illuminate the Church's action. In prayer, Jesus lived in uninterrupted contact with the Father in order to fulfil completely his plan of love for mankind.

## Jesus' first thirty years

Against the background of this extraordinary prayer Jesus lived his entire life in a family deeply tied to the religious tradition of the people of Israel. This is demonstrated by the references we find in the Gospels: his circumcision (cf. *Lk* 2:21), and his presentation in the temple (cf.

*Lk* 2:22-24), as well as his education and training at Nazareth, in the holy house (cf. *Lk* 2:39-40 and 2:51-52). This was "about thirty years" (*Lk* 3:23), a long period of hidden daily life, even though it included experiences of participation with the community in moments of religious expression, such as pilgrimages to Jerusalem (cf. *Lk* 2:41). In recounting the episode of the twelve-year-old Jesus in the temple, sitting among the teachers (cf. *Lk* 2:42-52), Luke the Evangelist makes us understand that Jesus, who prayed after his baptism in the Jordan, had a long-standing habit of intimate prayer to God the Father. This habit was rooted in the traditions and in the style of his family, and in his own crucial experiences within it. The twelve-year-old's answer to Mary and Joseph already suggests the divine Sonship which the heavenly voice expressed after his baptism: "How is it that you sought me? Did you not know that I must be in my Father's house?" (*Lk* 2:49). Jesus did not begin to pray after emerging from the waters of the Jordan, but continued in his ongoing, customary relationship with the Father; and it was in this close union with the Father that he stepped out of the hidden life in Nazareth into his public ministry.

## Jesus' prayer

Jesus' teaching on prayer certainly derives from the approach to prayer that he acquired in his family but its deep, essential origins are found in his being the Son of

God and in his unique relationship with God the Father. The *Compendium of the Catechism of the Catholic Church* answers the question: "*From whom did Jesus learn how to pray?*" in this way: "Jesus, with his human heart, learned how to pray from his Mother and from the Jewish tradition. But his prayer sprang from a more secret source because he is the eternal Son of God who in his holy humanity offers his perfect filial prayer to his Father" (n. 541).

In the Gospel narrative, the settings of Jesus' prayer are always placed halfway between integration into his people's tradition and the newness of a unique personal relationship with God. The "lonely place" (cf. *Mk* 1:35; *Lk* 5:16), to which he often withdrew, "the hills" he climbs in order to pray (cf. *Lk* 6:12; 9:28), "the night" that affords him solitude (cf. *Mk* 1:35; 6:46-47; *Lk* 6:12) recall moments in the process of God's revelation in the Old Testament, pointing out the continuity of his saving plan. Yet, at the same time, they mark moments of special importance for Jesus, who fits consciously into this plan, completely faithful to the Father's will.

In our prayer too we must learn, increasingly, to enter this history of salvation of which Jesus is the summit, to renew before God our personal decision to open ourselves to his will, to ask him for the strength to conform our will to his will, throughout our life, in obedience to his design of love for us.

## Prayer in the night

Jesus' prayer penetrates all the phases of his ministry and all his days. Difficulties do not obstruct it. The Gospels allow us a glimpse of Jesus' habit of spending part of the night in prayer. Mark the Evangelist tells of one of these nights, after the tiring day of the multiplication of the loaves, and writes: "Immediately he made his disciples get into the boat and go before him to the other side, to Bethsaida, while he dismissed the crowd. And after he had taken leave of them, he went into the hills to pray. And when evening came, the boat was out on the sea, and he was alone on the land" (*Mk* 6:45-47). When decisions became urgent and complicated his prayers grew longer and more intense. Just before he chose the Twelve Apostles, for example, Luke emphasises the nocturnal duration of Jesus' preparatory prayer: "In those days he went out into the hills to pray; and all night he continued in prayer to God. And when it was day, he called his disciples, and chose from them twelve, whom he named apostles: (*Lk* 6:12-13).

## Prayer today

In looking at Jesus' prayers, a question must arise within us: how do I pray? How do we pray? How much time do I give to my relationship with God? Are people today given sufficient education and formation in prayer? And who can teach it? In the Apostolic Exhortation *Verbum Domini* I spoke of the importance of the prayerful reading of Sacred

Scripture. In gathering what emerged at the Assembly of the Synod of Bishops, I placed a special emphasis on the specific form of *lectio divina*. Listening, meditating, and being silent before the Lord who speaks is an art which is learned by practising it with perseverance. Certainly, prayer is a gift which nevertheless asks to be accepted; it is a work of God but demands commitment and continuity on our part. Above all continuity and constancy are important. Jesus' exemplary experience itself shows that his prayer, enlivened by the fatherhood of God and by communion with the Spirit, was deepened and prolonged in faithful practice, up to the Garden of Olives and to the Cross.

## Our prayer

Today Christians are called to be witnesses of prayer precisely because our world is often closed to the divine horizon and to the hope that leads to the encounter with God. In deep friendship with Jesus and living in him and with him the filial relationship with the Father, through our constant and faithful prayer we can open windows on God's Heaven. Indeed, by taking the way of prayer, attaching no importance to human things, we can help others to take it. For Christian prayer too it is true that, in journeying on, new paths unfold.

Let us train ourselves in an intense relationship with God, with prayer that is not occasional but constant, full of faith, capable of illuminating our lives, as Jesus taught us. And let us ask him to enable us to communicate to people who are close to us, to those whom we meet on our way, the joy of the encounter with the Lord, Light for our existence. Many thanks.

# The Cry of Exultation

## Cry of Exultation

The Evangelists Matthew and Luke (cf. *Mt* 11:25-30 and *Lk* 10:21-22) have handed down to us a "jewel" of Jesus' prayer that is often called the *Cry of Exultation* or the *Cry of Messianic Exultation*. It is a prayer of thanksgiving and praise, as we have heard. In the original Greek of the Gospels the word with which this jubilation begins and which expresses Jesus' attitude in addressing the Father is *exomologoumai*, which is often translated as "I praise" (cf. *Mt* 11:25 and *Lk* 10:21). However, in the New Testament writings this term indicates mainly two things: the first is "to confess" fully - for example, John the Baptist asked those who went to him to be baptised to recognise their every sin (cf. *Mt* 3:6); the second thing is "to be in agreement". Therefore, the words with which Jesus begins his prayer contain his full recognition of the Father's action and, at the same time, his being in total, conscious and joyful agreement with this way of acting, with the Father's plan. The Cry of Exultation is the apex of a journey of prayer in which Jesus' profound and close communion with the life of the Father in the Holy Spirit clearly emerges and his divine sonship is revealed.

## The Son in communion with the Father

Jesus addresses God by calling him "Father". This word expresses Jesus' awareness and certainty of being "the Son" in intimate and constant communion with him, and this is the central focus and source of every one of Jesus' prayers. We see it clearly in the last part of the hymn which illuminates the entire text. Jesus said: "All things have been delivered to me by my Father; and no one knows who the Son is except the Father, or who the Father is except the Son and anyone to whom the Son chooses to reveal him" (*Lk* 10:22). Jesus was therefore affirming that only "the Son" truly knows the Father. All the knowledge that people have of each other - we all experience this in our human relationships - entails involvement, a certain inner bond between the one who knows and the one who is known, at a more or less profound level: we cannot know anyone without a communion of being. In the Cry of Exultation - as in all his prayers - Jesus shows that true knowledge of God presupposes communion with him. Only by being in communion with the other can I begin to know him; and so it is with God: only if I am in true contact, if I am in communion with him, can I also know him. True knowledge, therefore, is reserved to the "Son", the Only Begotten One who is in the bosom of the Father since eternity (cf. *Jn* 1:18), in perfect unity with him. The Son alone truly knows God, since he is in an intimate communion of being; only the Son can truly reveal who God is.

## Jesus can lead us to the Father

The name "Father" is followed by a second title, "Lord of heaven and earth". With these words, Jesus sums up faith in creation and echoes the first words of Sacred Scripture: "In the beginning God created the heavens and the earth" (*Gn* 1:1). In praying, he recalls the great biblical narrative of the history of God's love for man that begins with the act of creation. Jesus fits into this love story, he is its culmination and its fulfilment. Sacred Scripture is illumined through his experience of prayer and lives again in its fullest breadth: the proclamation of the mystery of God and the response of man transformed. Yet, through the expression: "Lord of heaven and earth", we can also recognise that in Jesus, the Revealer of the Father, the possibility for man to reach God is reopened.

Let us now ask ourselves: to whom does the Son want to reveal God's mysteries? At the beginning of the hymn Jesus expresses his joy because the Father's will is to keep these things hidden from the learned and the wise and to reveal them to little ones (cf. *Lk* 10:21). Thus in his prayer, Jesus manifests his communion with the Father's decision to disclose his mysteries to the simple of heart: the Son's will is one with the Father's.

## **"Little children"**

Divine revelation is not brought about in accordance with earthly logic, which holds that cultured and powerful

people possess important knowledge and pass it on to
simpler people, to little ones. God used a quite different
approach: those to whom his communication was addressed
were, precisely, "little children". This is the Father's will,
and the Son shares it with him joyfully. The *Catechism
of the Catholic Church* says: "His exclamation, 'Yes,
Father!' expresses the depth of his heart, his adherence to
the Father's 'good pleasure' echoing his mother's *Fiat* at
the time of his conception and prefiguring what he will
say to the Father in his agony. The whole prayer of Jesus
is contained in this loving adherence of his human heart
to the 'mystery of the will' of the Father (*Ep* 1:9)" (n.
2603). The invocation that we address to God in the Our
Father derives from this: "Thy will be done on earth as it
is in heaven": together with Christ and in Christ we too
ask to enter into harmony with the Father's will, thereby
also becoming his children. Thus Jesus, in this Cry of
Exultation, expresses his will to involve in his own filial
knowledge of God all those whom the Father wishes to
become sharers in it; and those who welcome this gift are
the "little ones".

But what does being "little" and simple mean? What
is the "littleness" that opens man to filial intimacy with
God so as to receive his will? What must the fundamental
attitude of our prayer be? Let us look at the Sermon on the
Mount, in which Jesus says: "Blessed are the pure in heart,
for they shall see God" (*Mt* 5:8). It is purity of heart that

permits us to recognise the face of God in Jesus Christ; it is having a simple heart like the heart of a child, free from the presumption of those who withdraw into themselves, thinking they have no need of anyone, not even God.

## A joyful prayer

It is also interesting to notice the occasion on which Jesus breaks into this hymn to the Father. In Matthew's Gospel narrative it is joyful because, in spite of opposition and rejection, there are "little ones" who accept his word and open themselves to the gift of faith in him. The Cry of Exultation is in fact preceded by the contrast between the praise of John the Baptist - one of the "little ones" who recognised God's action in Jesus Christ (cf. *Mt* 11:2-19) - and the reprimand for the disbelief of the lake cities "where most of his mighty works had been performed" (cf. *Mt* 11:20-24). Hence Matthew saw the Exultation in relation to the words with which Jesus noted the effectiveness of his word and action: "Go and tell John what you hear and see: the blind receive their sight and the lame walk, lepers are cleansed and the deaf hear, and the dead are raised up, and the poor have the good news of the Gospel preached to them. And blessed is he who takes no offence at me" (*Mt* 11:4-6).

St Luke also presented the Cry of Exultation in connection with a moment of development in the proclamation of the Gospel. Jesus sent out the "seventy-two" others (*Lk* 10:1) and they departed fearful of the possible failure of their mission. Luke also emphasised the rejection encountered in the cities where the Lord had preached and had worked miracles. Nonetheless the seventy-two disciples returned full of joy because their mission had met with success; they realised that human infirmities are overcome with the power of Jesus' word. Jesus shared their pleasure: "in that same hour", at that very moment, he rejoiced.

## Rejoicing and rest

There are still two elements that I would like to underline. Luke the Evangelist introduces the prayer with the annotation: Jesus "rejoiced in the Holy Spirit" (*Lk* 10:21). Jesus rejoiced from the depths of his being, in what counted most: his unique communion of knowledge and love with the Father, the fullness of the Holy Spirit. By involving us in his sonship, Jesus invites us too to open ourselves to the light of the Holy Spirit, since - as the Apostle Paul affirms - "we do not know how to pray as we ought, but the Spirit himself intercedes for us with sighs too deep for words… according to the will of God" (*Rm* 8:26-27), and reveals the Father's love to us. In Matthew's Gospel, following the Cry of Exultation, we find one of Jesus' most heartfelt appeals: "Come to me, all who labour and are heavy laden, and I will give you rest" (*Mt* 11:28). Jesus asks us to go to him, for he is true Wisdom, to him who is "gentle and lowly in heart". He offers us "his yoke", the way of the wisdom of the Gospel which is neither a doctrine to be learned nor an ethical system but rather a Person to follow: he himself, the Only Begotten Son in perfect communion with the Father.

## The need for God

We have experienced for a moment the wealth of this prayer of Jesus. With the gift of his Spirit we too can turn to God in prayer with the confidence of children, calling him by the name Father, "Abba". However, we must have the heart of little ones, of the "poor in spirit" (*Mt* 5:3) in order to recognise that we are not self-sufficient, that we are unable to build our lives on our own but need God, that we need to encounter him, to listen to him, to speak to him. Prayer opens us to receiving the gift of God, his wisdom, which is Jesus himself, in order to do the Father's will in our lives and thus to find rest in the hardships of our journey. Many thanks.

# The Prayer of Jesus Linked to His Miraculous Healing Action

Today I would like to reflect with you on the prayer of Jesus linked to his miraculous healing action. Various situations are presented in the Gospels in which Jesus prays while he contemplates the beneficial and healing work of God the Father who acts through him. This is a form of prayer which, once again, demonstrates his unique relationship of knowledge and communion with the Father, while Jesus lets himself be involved with deep human participation in the hardships of his friends, for example, those of Lazarus and his family or of the many poor and sick people to whom he seeks to give practical help.

## The healing of the deaf mute

A significant case is the healing of the deaf mute (cf. *Mk* 7:32-37). Mark the Evangelist's account shows that Jesus' healing action is connected with the intense relationship he had both with his neighbour - the sick man - and with the Father. The scene of the miracle is described carefully, in these words: "Taking him aside from the multitude privately, he put his fingers into his ears, and he spat and touched his tongue; and looking up to heaven, he sighed, and said to him, '*Ephphatha*', that is 'Be opened'" (*Mk* 7:33-34). Jesus wanted the healing to take place "aside from the multitude". This does not seem to be due solely to the fact that the miracle must be kept hidden from people to prevent them from making any restrictive or distorted interpretation of the Person of Jesus. The decision to take the sick man aside ensures that at the moment of his healing Jesus and the deaf mute are on their own, brought together in a unique relationship. With a single gesture the Lord touches the sick man's ears and tongue, that is, the specific sites of his infirmity. The intensity of Jesus' attention is also demonstrated in the unusual treatment that was part of the healing. He uses his fingers and even his saliva. And the fact that the Evangelist records the original word spoken by the Lord, '*Ephphatha*', in other words, 'Be opened', highlights the unusual character of the scene.

## Christ is compassionate

The central point of this episode however is the fact that when Jesus was about to work the healing, he directly sought his relationship with the Father. Indeed the account relates that "looking up to heaven, he sighed" (v. 34). Jesus' attention to and treatment of the sick man are linked by a profound attitude of prayer addressed to God. Moreover, his sighing is described with a verb which, in the New Testament, indicates he aspiration to something good which is still lacking (cf. *Rm* 8:23). Thus, as a whole, the narrative shows that it was his human involvement with the sick man that prompted Jesus to pray. His unique relationship with the Father and his identity as the Only Begotten Son surface once again. God's healing and beneficial action become present in him, through his Person. It is not by chance that the people's last remark after the miracle has been performed is reminiscent of the evaluation of the Creation at the beginning of the Book of Genesis: "He has done all things well" (*Mk* 7:37). Prayer clearly entered the healing action of Jesus as he looked up to heaven. The power that healed the deaf mute was certainly elicited by compassion for him but came from recourse to the Father. These two relationships interact: the human relationship of compassion with the man enters into the relationship with God, and thus becomes healing.

### Jesus' friend Lazarus

In the Johannine narrative of the raising of Lazarus this same dynamic is testified by an even greater proof (cf. *Jn* 11:1-44) Here too are interwoven, on the one hand, Jesus' bond with a friend and with his suffering and, on the other, his filial relationship with the Father. Jesus' human participation in Lazarus' case has some special features. His friendship with Lazarus is repeatedly mentioned throughout the account, as well as his relationship with Martha and Mary, the sisters of Lazarus. Jesus himself says: "Our friend Lazarus has fallen asleep, but I go to awake him out of sleep" (*Jn* 11:11). Jesus' sincere affection for his friend is also highlighted by Lazarus' sisters, as well as by the Jews (cf. *Jn* 11:3; 11:36). It is expressed in Jesus' deep distress at seeing the grief of Martha and Mary and of all Lazarus' friends; he finds relief by bursting into tears - so profoundly human - on approaching the tomb: "When Jesus saw her [Martha] weeping, and the Jews who came with her also weeping, he was deeply moved in spirit and troubled; and he said, 'Where have you laid him?' They said to him, 'Lord, come and see'. Jesus wept" (*Jn* 11:33-35).

## Communion with God's will

This bond of friendship and Jesus' participation in and distress at the sorrow of Lazarus' relatives and acquaintances, is connected throughout the narrative to a continuous, intense relationship with the Father. The event, from the outset, is interpreted by Jesus in relation to his own identity and mission and to the glorification that awaits him. In fact on hearing of Lazarus' illness he commented: "The illness is not unto death; it is for the glory of God, so that the Son of God may be glorified by means of it" (*Jn* 11:4). Jesus also hears the news of his friend's death with deep human sadness but always with a clear reference to his relationship with God and with the mission that God has entrusted to him; he says: "Lazarus is dead; and for your sake I am glad that I was not there, so that you

may believe" (*Jn* 11:14-15). The moment of Jesus' explicit
prayer to the Father at the tomb was the natural outlet for
all that had happened, which took place in the double key
of his friendship with Lazarus and his filial relationship
with God. Here too, the two relationships go hand in hand.
"And Jesus lifted up his eyes and said, 'Father, I thank you
that you have heard me'" (*Jn* 11:41): it was a *eucharist*.
The sentence shows that Jesus did not cease, even for an
instant, his prayer of petition for Lazarus' life. This prayer
continued, indeed, it reinforced his ties with his friend and,
at the same time strengthened Jesus' decision to remain in
communion with the Father's will, with his plan of love in
which Lazarus' illness and death were to be considered as
a place for the manifestation of God's glory.

### God's greatest gift

In reading this account each one of us is called to
understand that in our prayers of petition to the Lord we
must not expect an immediate fulfilment of what we ask,
of our own will. Rather, we must entrust ourselves to the
Father's will, interpreting every event in the perspective
of his glory, of his plan of love, which to our eyes is
often mysterious. For this reason we too must take part
in our prayers, petitions, praise and thanksgiving, even
when it seems to us that God is not responding to our real
expectations. Abandoning ourselves to God's love which
always precedes and accompanies us is one of the basic

attitudes for our dialogue with him. On Jesus' prayer in the account of the raising of Lazarus the *Catechism of the Catholic Church* comments: "Jesus' prayer, characterised by thanksgiving, reveals to us how to ask: before the gift is given, Jesus commits himself to the One who in giving gives himself. The Giver is more precious than the gift; he is the 'treasure'; in him abides his Son's heart; the gift is given 'as well' (cf. *Mt* 6:21, 33)" (n. 2604). To me this seems very important: before the gift is given, committing ourselves to the One who gives. The Giver is more precious than the gift. For us too, therefore, over and above what God bestows on us when we call on him, the greatest gift that he can give us is his friendship, his presence and his love. He is the precious treasure to ask for and to preserve for ever.

### Jesus prays to lead the people to God

The prayer that Jesus prays as the rock was rolled away from the entrance to Lazarus' tomb thus has a special and unexpected development. In fact, after thanking God the Father, he adds: "I knew that you hear me always, but I have said this on account of the people standing by, that they may believe that you sent me" (*Jn* 11:42). With his prayer Jesus wanted to lead people back to faith, to total trust in God and in his will, and he wanted to show that this God who so loved man and the world that he gave his Only Begotten Son (cf. *Jn* 3:16) is the God of Life, the

God who brings hope and can reverse humanly impossible situations. Therefore a believer's trusting prayer is a living testimony of God's presence in the world, of his concern for humankind, of his action with a view to bringing about his plan of salvation.

## God and neighbour

Jesus' two prayers on which we have meditated just now and which accompany the healing of the deaf mute and the raising of Lazarus, reveal that the deep connection between the love of God and love of one's neighbour must also come into our own prayer. In Jesus, true God and true man, attention to others, especially if they were needy and suffering, compassion at the sight of the sorrow of a family who were his friends, led him to address the Father in that fundamental relationship which directed his entire life. However, the opposite is also true: communion with the Father, constant dialogue with him, spurred Jesus to be uniquely attentive to practical situations of men so as to bring God's comfort and love to them. Human relationships lead us toward the relationship with God, and the relationship with God leads us back to our neighbour.

Our prayer opens the door to God who teaches us to come out of ourselves constantly, to make us capable of being close to others in order to bring them comfort, hope and light, especially at moments of trial. May the Lord grant that we be capable of increasingly more intense prayer, in order to strengthen our personal relationship with God the Father, to open our heart to the needs of those around us and to feel the beauty of being "sons in the Son", together with a great many brothers and sisters. Many thanks.

# Prayer and the Holy Family of Nazareth

Today's meeting is taking place in the atmosphere of Christmas, imbued with deep joy at the Birth of the Saviour. We have just celebrated this Mystery whose echo ripples through the Liturgy of all these days. It is a Mystery of Light that all people in every era can relive with faith and prayer. It is precisely through prayer that we become capable of drawing close to God with intimacy and depth. Therefore, bearing in mind the theme of prayer that I am developing in the Catecheses in this period, I would like to invite you to reflect today on the way that prayer was part of the life of the Holy Family of Nazareth. Indeed, the house of Nazareth is a school of prayer where one learns to listen, meditate on and penetrate the profound meaning of the manifestation of the Son of God, following the example of Mary, Joseph and Jesus.

## Silence

The Discourse of the Servant of God Paul VI during his Visit to Nazareth is memorable. The Pope said that at the school of the Holy Family we "understand why we must maintain a spiritual discipline, if we wish to follow the teaching of the Gospel and become disciples of Christ".

He added: "In the first place it teaches us silence. Oh! If only esteem for silence, a wonderful and indispensable spiritual atmosphere, could be reborn within us! Whereas we are deafened by the din, the noise and discordant voices in the frenetic, turbulent life of our time. O silence of Nazareth! Teach us to be steadfast in good thoughts, attentive to our inner life, ready to hear God's hidden inspiration clearly and the exhortations of true teachers" (*Discourse in Nazareth*, 5 January 1964).

## Presentation in the Temple

We can draw various ideas for prayer and for the relationship with God and with the Holy Family from the Gospel narratives of the infancy of Jesus. We can begin with the episode of the Presentation of Jesus in the Temple. St Luke tells how "when the time came for their purification according to the law of Moses", Mary and Joseph "brought him up to Jerusalem to present him to the Lord" (2:22). Like every Jewish family that observed the law, Jesus' parents went to the Temple to consecrate their first-born son to God and to make the sacrificial offering. Motivated by their fidelity to the precepts of the Law, they set out from Bethlehem and went to Jerusalem with Jesus who was only forty days old. Instead of a year-old lamb they presented the offering of ordinary families, namely, two turtle doves. The Holy Family's pilgrimage was one of faith, of the offering of gifts - a symbol of prayer - and of the encounter with the Lord whom Mary and Joseph already perceived in their Son Jesus.

## The Virgin Mary

Mary was an unequalled model of contemplation of Christ. The face of the Son belongs to her in a special way because he had been formed in her womb and had taken a human likeness from her. No one has contemplated Jesus as diligently as Mary. The gaze of her heart was already focused on him at the moment of the Annunciation, when she conceived him through the action of the Holy Spirit; in the following months she gradually became aware of his presence, until, on the day of his birth, her eyes could look with motherly tenderness upon the face of her son as she wrapped him in swaddling clothes and laid him in the manger. Memories of Jesus, imprinted on her mind and on her heart, marked every instant of Mary's existence. She lived with her eyes fixed on Christ and cherished his every word. St Luke says: "Mary kept all these things, pondering them in her heart" (2:19) and thus describes Mary's approach to the Mystery of the Incarnation which was to extend throughout her life: keeping these things, pondering on them in her heart. Luke is the Evangelist who acquaints us with Mary's heart, with her faith (cf. 1:45), her hope and her obedience (cf. 1:38) and, especially, with her interiority and prayer (cf. 1:46-56), her free adherence to Christ (cf. 1:55). And all this proceeded from the gift of the Holy Spirit who overshadowed her (cf. 1:35), as he was to come down on the Apostles in accordance with Christ's promise (cf. *Ac* 1:8). This image of Mary which St Luke gives us presents Our Lady as a model for every believer who cherishes and compares Jesus' words with his actions, a comparison which is always progress in the knowledge of Jesus.

## A new relationship with God through Mary

After Bl. Pope John Paul II's example (cf. Apostolic Letter *Rosarium Virginis Mariae*) we can say that the prayer of the Rosary is modelled precisely on Mary, because it consists in contemplating the mysteries of Christ in spiritual union with the Mother of the Lord. Mary's ability to live by God's gaze is, so to speak, contagious. The first to experience this was St Joseph. His humble and sincere love for his betrothed and his decision to join his life to Mary's attracted and introduced him, "a just man" (*Mt* 1:19), to a special intimacy with God. Indeed, with Mary and later, especially, with Jesus, he began a new way of relating to God, accepting him in his life, entering his project of salvation and doing his will. After trustfully complying with the Angel's instructions - "Do not fear to take Mary your wife" (*Mt* 1:20) - he took Mary to him and shared his life with her; he truly gave the whole of himself to Mary and to Jesus and this led him to perfect his response to the vocation he had received.

## Saint Joseph

As we know, the Gospel has not recorded any of Joseph's words: his is a silent and faithful, patient and hard-working presence. We may imagine that he too, like his wife and in close harmony with her, lived the years of Jesus' childhood and adolescence savouring, as it were, his presence in their family. Joseph fulfilled every aspect of his paternal role. He must certainly have taught Jesus to pray, together with Mary. In particular Joseph himself must have taken Jesus to the Synagogue for the rites of the Sabbath, as well as to Jerusalem for the great feasts of the people of Israel. Joseph, in accordance with the Jewish tradition, would have led the prayers at home both every day - in the morning, in the evening, at meals - and on the principal religious feasts. In the rhythm of the days he spent at Nazareth, in the simple home and in Joseph's workshop, Jesus learned to alternate prayer and work, as well as to offer God his labour in earning the bread the family needed.

## Passover pilgrimage

And lastly, there is another episode that sees the Holy Family of Nazareth gathered together in an event of prayer. When Jesus was twelve years old, as we have heard, he went with his parents to the Temple of Jerusalem. This episode fits into the context of pilgrimage, as St Luke stresses: "His parents went to Jerusalem every year at the feast of the Passover. And when he was twelve years old,

they went up according to custom" (2:41-42). Pilgrimage is
an expression of religious devotion that is nourished by and
at the same time nourishes prayer. Here, it is the Passover
pilgrimage, and the Evangelist points out to us that the
family of Jesus made this pilgrimage every year in order to
take part in the rites in the Holy City. Jewish families, like
Christian families, pray in the intimacy of the home but
they also pray together with the community, recognising
that they belong to the People of God, journeying on; and
the pilgrimage expresses exactly this state of the People of
God on the move. Easter is the centre and culmination of
all this and involves both the family dimension and that of
liturgical and public worship.

### "Father"

In the episode of the twelve-year-old Jesus, the first words
of Jesus are also recorded: "How is it that you sought me?
Did you not know that I must be in my Father's house?"
(2:49). After three days spent looking for him his parents
found him in the temple, sitting among the teachers,
listening to them and asking them questions (cf. 2:46).
His answer to the question of why he had done this to his
father and mother was that he had only done what the Son
should do, that is, to be with his Father. Thus he showed
who is the true Father, what is the true home, and that he
had done nothing unusual or disobedient. He had stayed
where the Son ought to be, that is, with the Father, and he

stressed who his Father was. The term "Father" therefore dominates the tone of this answer and the Christological mystery appears in its entirety. Hence, this word unlocks the mystery, it is the key to the mystery of Christ, who is the Son, and also the key to our mystery as Christians who are sons and daughters in the Son. At the same time Jesus teaches us to be children by being with the Father in prayer. The Christological mystery, the mystery of Christian existence, is closely linked to, founded on, prayer. Jesus was one day to teach his disciples to pray, telling them: When you pray say "Father". And, naturally, do not just say the word, say it with your life, learn to say it meaningfully with your life: "Father"; and in this way you will be true sons in the Son, true Christians.

## A model of the Church

It is important at this point, when Jesus was still fully integrated in the life of the Family of Nazareth, to note the resonance that hearing this word "Father" on Jesus' lips must have had in the hearts of Mary and Joseph. It is also important to hear Jesus reveal and emphasise who the Father is, to hear this word from the lips and from the knowledge of him who is the Only-Begotten Son and who for this very reason, chose to stay on for three days in the Temple, which is the "Father's house". We may imagine that from this time the life of the Holy Family must have been even more full of prayer since from the heart of Jesus the boy - then an adolescent and a young man - this deep meaning of the relationship with God the Father would not cease to spread and to be echoed in the hearts of Mary and Joseph. This episode shows us the real situation, the atmosphere of being with the Father. So it was that the Family of Nazareth became the first model of the Church in which, around the presence of Jesus and through his mediation, everyone experiences the filial relationship with God the Father which also transforms interpersonal, human relationships.

## Prayer in the family

Dear friends, because of these different aspects that I have outlined briefly in the light of the Gospel, the Holy Family is the icon of the domestic Church, called to pray together. The family is the domestic Church and must be the first school of prayer. It is in the family that children, from the tenderest age, can learn to perceive the meaning of God, thanks to the teaching and example of their parents: to live in an atmosphere marked by God's presence. An authentically Christian education cannot dispense with the experience of prayer. If one does not learn how to pray in the family it will later be difficult to bridge this gap. And so I would like to address to you the invitation to pray together as a family at the school of the Holy Family of Nazareth and thereby really to become of one heart and soul, a true family. Many thanks.

# Jesus' Prayer at the Last Supper

During our journey of reflection on Jesus' prayer as it is presented in the Gospels, I would like today to meditate on the particularly solemn moment of his prayer at the Last Supper.

## Christ wishes to prepare the disciples

The temporal and emotional background of the festive meal at which Jesus takes leave of his friends is the imminence of his death, which he feels is now at hand. For some time Jesus had been talking about his Passion and had also been seeking to involve his disciples increasingly in this prospect. The Gospel according to Mark tells that from the time when he set out for Jerusalem, in the villages of distant Caesarea Philippi, Jesus had begun "to teach them that the Son of man must suffer many things and be rejected by the elders and the chief priests and the scribes, and be killed, and after three days rise again" (*Mk* 8:31). In addition, in the very days when he was preparing to say goodbye to the disciples, the life of the people was marked by the imminence of the Passover, that is, the commemoration of Israel's liberation from Egypt. This liberation, lived in the past and expected in the present and in the future, is experienced again in family celebrations of the Passover. The Last Supper fits into this context, but with a basic innovation. Jesus looks at his Passion, death and Resurrection with full awareness. He wishes to spend this Supper, that has a quite special character and is different from other meals with his disciples; it is his Supper, in which he gives something entirely new: himself. In this way Jesus celebrates his Pasch, anticipating his Cross and his Resurrection.

### Why is the Last Supper different?

This new element is highlighted for us in the account of the Last Supper in the Gospel of John, who does not describe it as the Passover meal for the very reason that Jesus was intending to inaugurate something new, to celebrate his Pasch, which is of course linked to the events of the Exodus. Moreover, according to John, Jesus died on the Cross at the very moment when the Passover lambs were being sacrificed in the Temple.

What then is the key to this Supper? It is in the gestures of breaking bread, of distributing it to his followers and of sharing the cup of wine, with the words that accompany them, and in the context of prayer in which they belong; it is the institution of the Eucharist, it is the great prayer of Jesus and of the Church. However, let us now take a closer look.

## The words of Christ

First of all, the New Testament traditions of the Institution of the Eucharist (cf. *1 Co* 11:23-25; *Lk* 22:14-20; *Mk* 14:22-25; *Mt* 26:26-29), point to the prayer that introduces Jesus' acts and words over the bread and over the wine, by using two parallel and complementary verbs. Paul and Luke speak of *eucaristia*/thanksgiving: "And he took bread, and when *he had given thanks* he broke it and gave it to them" (*Lk* 22:19). Mark and Matthew, however, emphasise instead the aspect of *eulogia*/blessing: "He took bread, and *blessed*, and broke it, and gave it to them" (*Mk* 14:22). Both these Greek terms, *eucaristeìn* and *eulogeìn*, refer to the Hebrew *berakha*, that is, the great prayer of thanksgiving and blessing of Israel's tradition which inaugurated important feasts. The two different Greek words indicate the two intrinsic and complementary orientations of this prayer. *Berakha*, in fact, means primarily thanksgiving and praise that rise to God for the gift received: at the Last Supper of Jesus, it is a matter of bread - made from the wheat that God causes to sprout and grow in the earth - and wine, produced from the fruit that ripens on the vine. This prayer of praise and thanksgiving that is raised to God returns as a blessing that comes down from God upon the gift and enriches it. Thanking and praising God thus become blessing and the offering given to God returns to man blessed by the Almighty. The words of the Institution of the Eucharist fit into this context of prayer; in them the praise and blessing of the *berakha* become the blessing and transformation of the bread and wine into the Body and Blood of Jesus.

## The actions of Christ

Before the words of the Institution come the actions: the breaking of the bread and the offering of the wine. The one who breaks the bread and passes the cup is first of all the head of the family who welcomes his relatives to his table; but these gestures are also those of hospitality, of the welcome in convivial communion of the stranger who does not belong to the household. These very gestures, in the Supper with which Jesus takes leave of his followers, acquire a completely new depth. He gives a visible sign of the welcome to the banquet in which God gives himself. Jesus offers and communicates himself in the bread and in the wine.

## Christ gives himself freely

But how can all this happen? How can Jesus give himself at that moment? Jesus knows that his life is about to be taken from him in the torture of the Cross, the capital punishment of slaves, which Cicero described as *mors turpissima crucis* [a most cruel and disgraceful death]. With the gift of the bread and of the wine that he offers at the Last Supper, Jesus anticipates his death and his Resurrection, bringing about what he had said in his Good Shepherd Discourse: "I lay down my life, that I may take it again. No one takes it from me, but I lay it down of my own accord. I have power to lay it down, and I have power to take it again; this charge I have received from my Father" (*Jn* 10:17-18). He therefore offers in anticipation the life that will be taken from him and in this way transforms his violent death into a free act of giving himself for others and to others. The violence he suffered is transformed into an active, free and redemptive sacrifice.

## Celebrate with bread

Once again in prayer, begun in accordance with the ritual forms of the Biblical tradition, Jesus shows his identity and his determination to fulfil his mission of total love to the very end, and of offering in obedience to the Father's will. The profound originality of the gift of himself to his followers, through the Eucharistic memorial, is the culmination of the prayer that distinguishes his farewell supper. In contemplating Jesus' actions and words on that night, we see clearly that it is in this close and constant relationship with the Father that he carries out his act of bequeathing to his followers and to each one of us the sacrament of love, the "*Sacramentum caritatis*". The words: "Do this in remembrance of me" (*1 Co* 11:24, 25), ring out twice in the Upper Room. With the gift of himself he celebrates his Pasch, becoming the true Lamb that brings the whole of the ancient worship to fulfilment. For this reason St Paul, speaking to the Christians of Corinth, says: "Christ [our Pasch], our Paschal Lamb, has been sacrificed. Let us, therefore, celebrate the festival... with the unleavened bread of sincerity and truth" (*1 Co* 5:7-8).

## Jesus' prayer gives strength to the weak

Luke the Evangelist has retained a further precious element of the events of the Last Supper that enables us to see the moving depth of Jesus' prayer for his own on that night: his attention to each one. Starting with the prayer of thanksgiving and blessing, Jesus arrives at the Eucharistic gift, the gift of himself, and, while he is giving the crucial sacramental reality, he addresses Peter. At the end of the meal, he says: "Simon, Simon, behold, Satan demanded to have you, that he might sift you like wheat, but I have prayed for you that your faith may not fail; and when you have turned again, strengthen your brethren" (*Lk* 22:31-32). Jesus' prayer, when his disciples were about to be put to the test, helped them to overcome their weakness in their effort to understand that the way of God passes through the Paschal Mystery of the death and Resurrection, anticipated in the offering of the bread and the wine. The Eucharist is the food of pilgrims that also becomes strength for those who are weary, worn-out and bewildered. And the prayer was specially for Peter, so that once he had turned

again he might strengthen his brethren in the faith. Luke
the Evangelist recalls that it was the very gaze of Jesus in
seeking Peter's face at the moment when he had just denied
him three times which gave him the strength to continue
following in his footsteps: "And immediately, while he
was still speaking, the cock crowed. And the Lord turned
and looked at Peter. And Peter remembered the word of the
Lord" (*Lk* 22:60-61).

## United with Christ in prayer

By participating in the Eucharist, we experience in an
extraordinary manner the prayer that Jesus prayed and
prays ceaselessly for every person so that the evil which
we all encounter in life may not get the upper hand and that
the transforming power of Christ's death and Resurrection
may act within us. In the Eucharist the Church responds
to Jesus' commandment: "Do this in remembrance of
me" (*Lk* 22:19; cf. *1 Co* 11:24-26); she repeats the prayer
of thanksgiving and praise and, with it, the words of the
transubstantiation of the bread and wine into the Body and
Blood of the Lord. Our Eucharists are: being attracted at
this moment of prayer, being united ever anew to Jesus'
prayer. From the outset, the Church has understood the
words of consecration as part of the *prayer prayed together
to Jesus*; as a central part of the praise filled with gratitude,
through which the fruits of the earth and the work of man
come to us anew, given by God as the Body and Blood of

Jesus; as the self-giving of God himself in his Son's self-emptying love (cf. *Jesus of Nazareth*, II, Ignatius Press, San Francisco, 2011, p. 128). Participating in the Eucharist, nourishing ourselves with the Flesh and Blood of the Son of God, we join our prayers to that of the Paschal Lamb on his supreme night, so that our life may not be lost despite our weakness and our unfaithfulness, but be transformed.

Dear friends, let us ask the Lord that after being duly prepared, also with the sacrament of Penance, our participation in his Eucharist, indispensable to Christian life, may always be the highest point in all our prayer. Let us ask that we too, profoundly united in his offering to the Father, may transform our own crosses into a free and responsible sacrifice of love for God and for our brethren. Many thanks.

# On the Priestly Prayer of Jesus

In today's Catechesis let us focus our attention on the prayer that Jesus raises to the Father in the "Hour" of his exaltation and glorification (cf. *Jn* 17:1-26). As the *Catechism of the Catholic Church* says: "Christian Tradition rightly calls this prayer the 'priestly' prayer of Jesus. It is the prayer of our High Priest, inseparable from his sacrifice, from his "passing over" (Passover) to the Father to whom he is wholly 'consecrated'" (n. 2747).

## *Yom Kippur*

The extreme richness of Jesus' prayer can be understood especially if we set it against the backdrop of the Jewish feast of expiation, *Yom Kippur*. On that day the High Priest makes expiation first for himself and then for the priests, and, lastly, for the whole community of the people. The purpose is to restore to the People of Israel, after a year's transgressions, the awareness of their reconciliation with God, the awareness that they are the Chosen People, a "holy people", among the other peoples. The prayer of Jesus, presented in Chapter 17 of the Gospel according to John, returns to the structure of this feast. On that night Jesus addresses the Father at the moment when he is offering himself. He, priest and victim, prays for himself, for the Apostles and for all those who will believe in him and for the Church of all time (cf. *Jn* 17:20).

## Jesus prays for glorification

The prayer that Jesus prays for himself is the request for his glorification, for his "exaltation" in his "Hour". In fact, it is more than a prayer of petition, more than the declaration of his full willingness to enter, freely and generously, into the plan of God the Father, which is fulfilled in his being consigned and in his death and Resurrection. This "Hour" began with Judas' betrayal (cf. 13:31) and was to end in the ascension of the Risen Jesus to the Father (*Jn* 20:17). Jesus comments on Judas' departure from the Upper Room with these words: "Now is the Son of man glorified, and in him God is glorified" (*Jn* 13:31). It is not by chance that he begins his priestly prayer saying: "Father, the hour has come; glorify your Son that the Son may glorify you" (*Jn* 17:1). The glorification that Jesus asks for himself as High Priest is the entry into full obedience to the Father, an obedience that leads to his fullest filial condition: "And now, Father, glorify me in your own presence with the glory which I had with you before the world was made" (*Jn* 17:5). This readiness and this request are the first act of the new priesthood of Jesus, which is a total gift of himself on the Cross, and on the Cross itself - the supreme act of love - he is glorified because love is the true glory, the divine glory.

## Manifestation

The second moment of this prayer is the intercession that
Jesus makes for the disciples who have been with him.
They are those of whom Jesus can say to the Father: "I
have manifested your name to the men whom you gave
me out of the world; yours they were, and you gave them
to me, and they have kept your word" (*Jn* 17:6). This
"manifesting God's name to men" is the fulfilment of a new
presence of the Father among the people, for humanity.
This "manifesting" is not only a *word*, but is *reality* in
Jesus; God is with us, and so his name - his presence with
us, his being one of us - is "fulfilled". This manifestation
is thus realised in the Incarnation of the Word. In Jesus
God enters human flesh, he becomes close in a new and
unique way. And this presence culminates in the sacrifice
that Jesus makes in his Pasch of death and Resurrection.

### Jesus prays for consecration of the disciples

At the centre of this prayer of intercession and of expiation
in favour of the disciples is the request for *consecration*;
Jesus says to the Father: "They are not of the world, even
as I am not of the world. Sanctify them in the truth; your
word is truth. As you did send me into the world, so I have
sent them into the world. And for their sake I consecrate
myself, that they also may be consecrated in truth" (*Jn*
17:16-19). I ask: what does "consecrate" mean in this
case? First of all it must be said that really only God is

"consecrated" or "holy". "To consecrate" therefore means "to transfer" a reality - a person or a thing - to become the property of God. And two complementary aspects are present in this: on the one hand, removing them from ordinary things, segregating, "setting them apart" from the context of personal human life so that they may be totally given to God; and on the other, this segregation, this transferral into God's sphere, has the very meaning of "sending", of mission: precisely because he or she is given to God, the reality, the consecrated person, exists "for" others, is given to others. Giving to God means no longer existing for oneself, but for everyone. Whoever, like Jesus, is segregated from the world and set apart for God with a view to a task is, for this very reason, fully available to all. For the disciples the task will be to continue Jesus' mission, to be given to God and thereby to be on mission for all. The Risen One, appearing to his disciples on Easter evening, was to say to them: "Peace be with you. As the Father has sent me, even so I send you" (*Jn* 20:21).

## Jesus prays for the Church

The third part of this priestly prayer extends to the end of time. In it Jesus turns to the Father in order to intercede for all those who will be brought to the faith through the mission inaugurated by the Apostles and continued in history: "I do not pray for these only, but also for those who believe in me through their word". Jesus prays for the Church of all time, he also prays for us (*Jn* 17:20). The Catechism of the Catholic Church comments: "Jesus fulfilled the work of the Father completely; his prayer, like his sacrifice, extends until the end of time. The prayer of this hour fills the end-times and carries them toward their consummation" (n. 2749).

## Jesus' prayer is for unity

The central request of the priestly prayer of Jesus dedicated to his disciples of all epochs is that of the future unity of those who will believe in him. This unity is not a worldly product. It comes exclusively from the divine unity and reaches us from the Father, through the Son and in the Holy Spirit. Jesus invokes a gift that comes from Heaven and has its effect - real and perceptible - on earth. He prays "that they may all be one; even as you, Father are in me, and I in you, that they also may be in us, so that the world may believe that you have sent me" (*Jn* 17:21). Christian unity, on the one hand, is a secret reality that is in the heart of believers. But, at the same time, it must appear with full clarity in history; it must appear so that the world may believe; it has a very practical and concrete purpose: it must appear so that all may really be one. The unity of future disciples, in being united with Jesus - whom the Father sent into the world - is also the original source of the efficacy of the Christian mission in the world.

## The Church and the world

"We can say that the founding of the Church takes place" in the priestly prayer of Jesus. In this very place, in the act of the Last Supper, Jesus creates the Church. "For what else is the Church, if not the community of disciples who through faith in Jesus Christ as the one sent by the Father", receives his unity and is involved in Jesus' mission to save the world, leading it to knowledge of God? Here we really find a true definition of the Church. "The Church is born from Jesus' prayer. But this prayer is more than words; it is the act by which he 'sanctifies' himself, that is to say, he 'sacrifices' himself for the life of the world" (cf. *Jesus of Nazareth*, II, Ignatius Press, San Francisco, 2011, p. 101).

Jesus prays that his disciples may be one. By virtue of this unity, received and preserved, the Church can walk "in the world" without being "of the world" (cf. *Jn* 17:16) and can live the mission entrusted to her so that the world may believe in the Son and in the Father who sent him. Therefore the Church becomes the place in which the mission of Christ itself continues: to lead the "world" out of man's alienation from God and from himself, out of sin, so that it may return to being the world of God.

## Pray as Christ did

We have grasped a few elements of the great richness of the priestly prayer of Jesus, which I invite you to read and to meditate on so that it may guide us in dialogue with the Lord and teach us to pray. Let us too, therefore, in our prayers, ask God to help us to enter, more fully, into the design he has for each one of us. Let us ask to be "consecrated" to him, to belong to him more and more, to be able to love others more and more, those who are near and far; let us ask to be able always to open our prayer to the dimensions of the world, not closing it to the request for help with our problems but remembering our neighbour before the Lord, learning the beauty of interceding for others; let us ask for the gift of visible unity among all believers in Christ - we have invoked it forcefully in this Week of Prayer for Christian Unity - let us pray to be ever ready to answer anyone who asks us to account for the hope that is in us (cf. *1 P* 3:15). Many thanks.

# Jesus' Prayer at Gethsemane

Today I would like to talk about Jesus' prayer in the Garden of Olives at Gethsemane. The setting of the Gospel narrative of this prayer is particularly significant. Jesus sets out for the Mount of Olives after the Last Supper while he is praying together with his disciples. The Evangelist Mark says: "When they had sung a hymn, they went out to the Mount of Olives" (*Mk* 14:26). This is probably an allusion to singing one of the *Hallel* Psalms, with which thanks are given to God for the liberation of the People from slavery and his help is asked for the ever new difficulties and threats of the present. The walk to Gethsemane is punctuated by remarks from Jesus that convey a sense of his impending death and proclaim the imminent dispersion of the disciples.

## Jesus wants the disciples to go with him

Having reached the grove on the Mount of Olives, that night too Jesus prepares for personal prayer. However, this time something new happens: it seems that he does not want to be left alone. Jesus would often withdraw from the crowd and from the disciples themselves "to a lonely place" (*Mk* 1:35) or he would go up "into the hills", St Mark says (cf. *Mk* 6:46). Instead at Gethsemane he invites Peter, James and John to stay closer to him. They are the

disciples he called upon to be with him on the Mount of
the Transfiguration (cf. *Mk* 9:2-13). This closeness of the
three during his prayer in Gethsemane is important. On
that night too Jesus was going to pray to the Father "apart",
for his relationship with the Father is quite unique: it is
the relationship of the Only-Begotten Son. Indeed, one
might say that, especially on that night, no one could really
have come close to the Son, who presented himself to the
Father with his absolutely unique and exclusive identity.
Yet, although Jesus arrives "alone" at the place in which
he was to stop and pray, he wants at least three disciples to
be near him, to be in a closer relationship with him. This
is a spatial closeness, a plea for solidarity at the moment
in which he feels death approaching, but above all it is a
closeness in prayer, in order to express in a certain way
harmony with him at the moment when he is preparing to
do the Father's will to the very end; and it is an invitation
to every disciple to follow him on the Way of the Cross.
Mark the Evangelist recounts: "He took with him Peter
and James and John, and began to be greatly distressed and
troubled. And he said to them '*My soul is very sorrowful*,
even to death; remain here, and watch'" (14:33-34).

### The will of God is difficult

In the words he addresses to the three, Jesus once again
expresses himself in the language of the Psalms: "*My soul
is very sorrowful*", an expression borrowed from Psalm

43 (cf. *Ps* 43[42]:5). The firm determination "unto death" thus calls to mind a situation lived by many of those sent by God in the Old Testament and which is expressed in their prayers. Indeed, following the mission entrusted to them frequently means encountering hostility, rejection and persecution. Moses is dramatically aware of the trial he is undergoing while guiding the people through the desert, and says to God: "I am not able to carry all this people alone, the burden is too heavy for me. If you will deal thus with me, rather kill me at once, kill me if I have found favour in your sight, that I may not see my wretchedness" (cf. *Nb* 11:14-15). Elijah too finds doing his duty to God and to his People difficult. The first Book of Kings recounts: "He himself went a day's journey into the wilderness, and came and sat under a broom tree; and he asked that he might die, saying, 'It is enough; now, O Lord, take away my life; for I am no better than my fathers'" (19:4).

What Jesus says to the three disciples whom he wants near him during his prayer at Gethsemane shows that he feels fear and anguish in that "Hour", experiencing his last profound loneliness precisely while God's plan is being brought about. Moreover Jesus' fear and anguish sums up the full horror of man in the face of his own death, the certainty that it is inescapable and a perception of the burden of evil that touches our lives.

### Abandonment in the Father

After the invitation to stay with him to watch and pray which he addresses to the three, Jesus speaks to the Father "alone". Mark the Evangelist tells us that "going a little farther, he fell on the ground and prayed that, if it were possible, the hour might pass from him" (14:35). Jesus fell prostrate on the ground: a position of prayer that expresses obedience to the Father and abandonment in him with complete trust. This gesture is repeated at the beginning of the celebration of the Passion, on Good Friday, as well as in monastic profession and in the ordination of deacons, priests and bishops in order to express, in prayer, corporally too, complete entrustment to God, trust in him. Jesus then asks the Father, if this be possible, to obtain that this hour pass from him. It is not only man's fear and anguish in the face of death, but it is the devastation of the Son of God who perceives the terrible mass of evil that he must take upon himself to overcome it, to deprive it of power.

Dear friends, in prayer we too should be able to lay before God our labours, the suffering of certain situations, of certain days, the daily commitment to following him, to being Christian, and also the weight of the evil that we see within ourselves and around us, so that he may give us hope and make us feel his closeness and give us a little light on the path of life.

## Jesus prays to his Father

Jesus continues his prayer: "*Abba*, Father, all things are possible to you; remove this cup from me; yet not what I will, but what you will" (*Mk* 14:36). In this invocation there are three revealing passages. At the beginning we have the double use of the word with which Jesus addresses God: "*Abba*! Father!" (*Mk* 14:36a). We know well that the Aramaic word *Abbà* is the term that children use to address their father and hence that it expresses Jesus' relationship with God, a relationship of tenderness, affection, trust and abandonment. The second element is found in the central part of the invocation: awareness of the Father's omnipotence - "all things are possible to you" - which introduces a request in which, once again, the drama of Jesus' human will appears as he faces death and evil: "remove this cup from me!" However, there is the third expression in Jesus' prayer, and it is the crucial one, in which the human will adheres to the divine will without reserve. In fact, Jesus ends by saying forcefully: "yet not what I will but what you will" (*Mk* 14:36c). In the unity of the divine person of the Son, the human will finds its complete fulfilment in the total abandonment of the I to the You of the Father, called Abba.

## Human will and divine will

St Maximus the Confessor says that ever since the moment of the creation of man and woman, the human will has been oriented to the divine will and that it is precisely in the "yes" to God that the human will is fully free and finds its fulfilment. Unfortunately, because of sin, this "yes" to God is transformed into opposition: Adam and Eve thought that the "no" to God was the crowning point of freedom, of being fully themselves. On the Mount of Olives, Jesus brings the human will back to the unreserved "yes" to God; in him the natural will is fully integrated in the orientation that the Divine Person gives it. Jesus lives his life in accordance with the centre of his Person: his being the Son of God. His human will is drawn into the "I" of the Son who abandons himself totally to the Father. Thus Jesus tells us that it is only by conforming our own will to the divine one that human beings attain their true height, that they become "divine"; only by coming out of ourselves, only in the "yes" to God, is Adam's desire - and the desire of us all - to be completely free realised. It is what Jesus brings about at Gethsemane: in transferring the human will into the divine will the true man is born and we are redeemed.

## The teaching of the Church

The *Compendium of the Catechism of the Catholic Church* teaches concisely: "The prayer of Jesus during his agony in the Garden of Gethsemane and his last words on the Cross reveal the depth of his filial prayer. Jesus brings to completion the loving plan of the Father and takes upon himself all the anguish of humanity and all the petitions

and intercessions of the history of salvation. He presents
them to the Father who accepts them and answers them
beyond all hope by raising his Son from the dead" (n.
543). Truly "nowhere else in Sacred Scripture do we gain
so deep an insight into the inner mystery of Jesus as in
the prayer on the Mount of Olives (*Jesus of Nazareth*, II,
Ignatius Press, San Francisco, 2011, p. 157).

### "Thy will be done"

Every day in the prayer of the Our Father we ask the Lord:
"Thy will be done, on earth as it is in heaven" (*Mt* 6:10). In
other words we recognise that there is a will of God with
us and for us, a will of God for our life that must become
every day, increasingly, the reference of our willing and
of our being; we recognise moreover that "heaven" is
where God's will is done and where the "earth" becomes
"heaven", a place where love, goodness, truth and divine
beauty are present, only if, on earth, God's will is done. In
Jesus' prayer to the Father on that terrible and marvellous
night in Gethsemane, the "earth" became "heaven"; the
"earth" of his human will, shaken by fear and anguish, was
taken up by his divine will in such a way that God's will
was done on earth. And this is also important in our own
prayers: we must learn to entrust ourselves more to divine
Providence, to ask God for the strength to come out of
ourselves to renew our "yes" to him, to say to him "thy will
be done", so as to conform our will to his. It is a prayer we

must pray every day because it is not always easy to entrust ourselves to God's will, repeating the "yes" of Jesus, the "yes" of Mary. The Gospel accounts of Gethsemane regretfully show that the three disciples, chosen by Jesus to be close to him, were unable to watch with him, sharing in his prayer, in his adherence to the Father, and they were overcome by sleep. Dear friends, let us ask the Lord to enable us to keep watch with him in prayer, to follow the will of God every day even if he speaks of the Cross, to live in ever greater intimacy with the Lord, in order to bring a little bit of God's "heaven" to this "earth". Many thanks.

# Jesus' Prayer in the Face of Death
## (Matthew and Mark)

Today I would like to reflect with you on the prayer of Jesus when death was imminent, pausing to think about everything St Mark and St Matthew tell us. The two Evangelists record the prayer of the dying Jesus not only in Greek, in which their accounts are written, but, because of the importance of these words, also in a mixture of Hebrew and Aramaic. In this way they have passed down not only the content but also the sound that this prayer had on Jesus' lips: let us really listen to Jesus' words as they were. At the same time, the Evangelists describe to us the attitude of those present at the crucifixion who did not understand - or did not want to understand - this prayer.

### Jesus' six hours on the Cross

St Mark wrote, as we have heard: "When the sixth hour had come, there was darkness over the whole land until the ninth hour. And at the ninth hour Jesus cried with a loud voice, '*Eloi, Eloi, lama sabachthani?*' which means, 'My God, my God, why have you forsaken me?'" (15:33-34). In the structure of the account, the prayer - Jesus' cry - is raised at the end of the three hours of darkness that shrouded all the earth from midday until three o'clock in the afternoon. These three hours of darkness are in turn the continuation of a previous span of time, also of three hours, that began with the crucifixion of Jesus. The Evangelist Mark, in fact, tells us that "it was the third hour, when they crucified him" (15:25). Taking the times given in the narrative, Jesus' six hours on the Cross are divided into two parts of equal length.

**Three hours of mockery and three hours of darkness**

The mockery of various groups, which displays their scepticism and confirms their disbelief, fits into the first three hours, from nine o'clock in the morning until midday. St Mark writes: "Those who passed by derided him" (15:29); "So also the chief priests mocked him to one another with the scribes" (15:31); "Those who were crucified with him also reviled him" (15:32). In the following three hours, from midday until "the ninth hour" [three o'clock in the afternoon], the Evangelist speaks only of the darkness that had come down over the entire earth; only darkness fills the whole scene without any references to people's movements or words. While Jesus is drawing ever closer to death, there is nothing but darkness that covers "the whole land".

**God is present in the darkness**

The cosmos also takes part in this event: the darkness envelops people and things, but even at this moment of darkness God is present, he does not abandon them. In the biblical tradition darkness has an ambivalent meaning: it is a sign of the presence and action of evil, but also of a mysterious presence and action of God who can triumph over every shadow. In the Book of Exodus, for example, we read "The Lord said to Moses: "Lo, I am coming to you in a thick cloud" (19:9); and, further: "the people stood afar off, while Moses drew near to the thick darkness where God was" (20:21). And in his discourses in Deuteronomy, Moses recounts: "And you came near and stood at the foot of the mountain, while the mountain burned with fire to the heart of heaven wrapped in darkness, cloud, and gloom" (4:11); you "heard the voice out of the midst of the darkness, while the mountain was burning with fire" (5:23). In the scene of the crucifixion of Jesus the darkness engulfs the earth and the Son of God immerses himself in the shadows of death in order to bring life, with his act of love.

## The voice of God

Returning to St Mark's narrative, in the face of the insults of various categories of people, in the face of the pall of darkness that shrouds everything, at the moment when he faces death, Jesus, with the cry of his prayer, shows that with the burden of suffering and death in which there seems to be abandonment, the absence of God, he is utterly certain of the closeness of the Father who approves this supreme act of love, the total gift of himself, although the voice from on high is not heard, as it was on other occasions.

In reading the Gospels we realise that in other important passages on his earthly existence Jesus had also seen the explanatory voice of God associated with the signs of the Father's presence and approval of his journey of love. Thus in the event that follows the Baptism in the Jordan, at the tearing open of the heavens, the words of the Father had been heard: "Thou art my beloved Son, with thee I am well pleased" (*Mk* 1:11). Then in the Transfiguration, the sign of the cloud was accompanied with these words: "This is my beloved Son; listen to him" (*Mk* 9:7). Instead, at the approach of the death of the Crucified One, silence falls, no voice is heard, but the Father's loving gaze is fixed on his Son's gift of love.

### Jesus cries out for God

However, what is the meaning of Jesus' prayer, of the cry he addresses to the Father: "My God, my God, why have you forsaken me?": doubt about his mission, about the Father's presence? Might there not be in this prayer the knowledge that he had been forsaken? The words that Jesus addresses to the Father are the beginning of Psalm 22[21], in which the Psalmist expresses to God his being torn between feeling forsaken and the certain knowledge of God's presence in his People's midst. He, the Psalmist, prays: "O my God, I cry by day, but you do not answer; and by night, but find no rest. Yet you are holy, enthroned on the praises of Israel" (vv. 3-4). The Psalmist speaks of this "cry" in order to express the full suffering of his prayer to God, seemingly absent: in the moment of anguish his prayer becomes a cry.

This also happens in our relationship with the Lord: when we face the most difficult and painful situations, when it seems that God does not hear, we must not be afraid to entrust the whole weight of our overburdened hearts to him, we must not fear to cry out to him in our suffering, we must be convinced that God is close, even if he seems silent.

## Jesus takes upon himself our sin

Repeating from the Cross the first words of Psalm 22[21] "*Eli, Eli, lama sabachthani?*" - "My God, my God, why have you forsaken me?" (*Mt* 27:46), uttering the words of the Psalm, Jesus prays at the moment of his ultimate rejection by men, at the moment of abandonment; yet he prays, with the Psalm, in the awareness of God's presence, even in that hour when he is feeling the human drama of death. However, a question arises within us: how is it possible that such a powerful God does not intervene to save his Son from this terrible trial? It is important to understand that Jesus' prayer is not the cry of one who meets death with despair, nor is it the cry of one who knows he has been forsaken. At this moment Jesus makes his own the whole of Psalm 22[21], the Psalm of the suffering People of Israel. In this way he takes upon himself not only the sin of his people, but also that of all men and women who are suffering from the oppression of evil and, at the same time, he places all this before God's own heart, in the certainty that his cry will be heard in the Resurrection: "The cry of extreme anguish is at the same time the certainty of an answer from God, the certainty of salvation - not only for Jesus himself, but for 'many'" (*Jesus of Nazareth*, II, Ignatius Press, San Francisco, 2011, pp. 213-214).

## Jesus prays in our name

In this prayer of Jesus are contained his extreme trust and his abandonment into God's hands, even when God seems absent, even when he seems to be silent, in accordance with a plan that is incomprehensible to us. In the *Catechism of the Catholic Church* we read: "In the redeeming love that always united him to the Father, he assumed us in the state of our waywardness of sin, to the point that he could say in our name from the Cross: 'My God, my God, why have you forsaken me?'" (n. 603). His is a suffering in communion with us and for us, which derives from love and already bears within it redemption, the victory of love. The bystanders at the foot of the Cross of Jesus fail to understand, thinking that his cry is a supplication addressed to Elijah. In the scene they seek to assuage his thirst in order to prolong his life and to find out whether Elijah will truly come to his aid, but a loud cry brings the earthy life of Jesus, and their desire, to an end.

## God does not abandon us

In the final moment Jesus gives vent to his heart's grief, but at the same time makes clear the meaning of the Father's presence and his consent to the Father's plan of salvation of humanity. We too have to face ever anew the "today" of suffering of God's silence - we express it so often in our prayers - but we also find ourselves facing the "today" of the Resurrection, of the response of God who took upon himself our sufferings, to carry them together with us and to give us the firm hope that they will be overcome (cf. Encyclical Letter *Spe Salvi*, nn. 35-40).

Dear friends, let us lay our daily crosses before God in our prayers, in the certainty that he is present and hears us. Jesus' cry reminds us that in prayer we must surmount the barriers of our "ego" and our problems and open ourselves to the needs and suffering of others. May the prayer of Jesus dying on the Cross teach us to pray lovingly for our many brothers and sisters who are oppressed by the weight of daily life, who are living through difficult moments, who are in pain, who have no word of comfort; let us place all this before God's heart, so that they too may feel the love of God who never abandons us. Many thanks.

# On the Three Last "Words" of Jesus Dying on the Cross (Luke)

At our school of prayer last Wednesday I spoke of Jesus' prayer on the Cross, taken from Psalm 22[21]: "My God, my God, why have you forsaken me?" I would now like to continue to meditate on the prayer of Jesus on the Cross in the imminence of death. Today, I would like to reflect on the account we find in St Luke's Gospel. The Evangelist has passed down to us three "words" spoken by Jesus on the Cross, two of which - the first and the third - are prayers explicitly addressed to the Father. The second, on the other hand, consists of the promise made to the so-called "good thief" crucified with him; indeed, in response to the thief's entreaty, Jesus reassures him: "Truly, I say to you, today you will be with me in Paradise" (*Lk* 23:43). Thus in Luke's narrative the two prayers that the dying Jesus addresses to the Father and his openness to the supplication addressed to him by the repentant sinner are evocatively interwoven. Jesus calls on the Father and at the same time listens to the prayer of this man who is often called *latro poenitens*, "the repentant thief".

## "Father, forgive them"

Let us reflect on these three prayers of Jesus. He prays the first one immediately after being nailed to the Cross, while the soldiers are dividing his garments between them as a wretched reward for their service. In a certain sense the process of the Crucifixion ends with this action. St Luke writes: "When they came to the place which is called The Skull, there they crucified him, and the criminals, one on the right and one on the left. And Jesus said, 'Father, forgive them; for they know not what they do'. And they cast lots to divide his garments" (23:33-34). The first prayer that Jesus addresses to the Father is a prayer of intercession; he asks for forgiveness for his executioners. By so doing, Jesus is doing in person what he had taught in the Sermon on the Mount when he said: "I say to you that hear, Love your enemies, do good to those who hate you" (*Lk* 6:27); and he had also promised to those who are able to forgive: "Your reward will be great, and you will be sons of the Most High" (v. 35). Now, from the Cross he not only pardons his executioners but he addresses the Father directly, interceding for them.

## Forgiveness for ignorance

Jesus' attitude finds a moving "imitation" in the account of the stoning of St Stephen, the first martyr. Indeed Stephen, now nearing his end, "knelt down and cried with a loud voice, 'Lord, do not hold this sin against them'. And when he had said this, he fell asleep" (*Ac* 7:60): these were his last words. The comparison between Jesus' prayer for forgiveness and that of the protomartyr is significant. St Stephen turns to the Risen Lord and requests that his killing - an action described clearly by the words "this sin" - not be held against those who stoned him. Jesus on the Cross addresses the Father and not only asks forgiveness for those who crucify him but also offers an interpretation of what is happening. According to what he says, in fact, the men who are crucifying him "know not what they do" (*Lk* 23:34). He therefore postulates ignorance, "not knowing", as a reason for his request for the Father's forgiveness, because it leaves the door open to conversion, as, moreover, happens in the words that the centurion was to speak at Jesus' death: "Certainly this man was innocent" (v. 47), he was the Son of God. "It remains a source of comfort for all times and for all people that both in the case of those who genuinely did not know (his executioners) and in the case of those who did know (the people who condemned him), the Lord makes ignorance the motive for his plea for forgiveness: he sees it as a door that can open us to conversion" (*Jesus of Nazareth*, II, Ignatius Press, San Francisco, 2011, p. 208).

## A word of hope

The second "word" spoken by Jesus on the Cross recorded by St Luke is one of hope, it is his answer to the prayer of one of the two men crucified with him. The good thief comes to his senses before Jesus and repents, he realises he is facing the Son of God who makes the very Face of God visible, and begs him; "Jesus, remember me when you come in your kingly power" (v. 42). The Lord's answer to this prayer goes far beyond the request; in fact he says: "Truly, I say to you, today you will be with me in Paradise" (v. 43). Jesus knows that he is entering into direct communion with the Father and reopening to man the way to God's paradise. Thus, with this response, he gives the firm hope that God's goodness can also touch us, even at the very last moment of life, and that sincere prayer, even after a misspent life, encounters the open arms of the good Father who awaits the return of his son.

## Jesus' death in Heaven and on earth

However, let us consider the last words of Jesus dying. The Evangelists tells us: "It was now about the sixth hour, and there was darkness over the whole land until the ninth hour, while the sun's light failed; and the curtain of the temple was torn in two. Then Jesus, crying with a loud voice, said, 'Father, into your hands I commit my spirit!' And having said this he breathed his last" (vv. 44-46). Certain aspects of this narrative differ from the scene as described in Mark and in Matthew. The three hours of darkness are not described in Mark, whereas in Matthew they are linked with a series of different apocalyptic events such as the quaking of the earth, the opening of the tombs, the dead who are raised (cf. *Mt* 27:51-53). In Luke, the hours of darkness are caused by the eclipse of the sun, but the veil of the temple is torn at that moment. In this way Luke's account presents two signs, in a certain way parallel, in the heavens and in the temple. The heavens lose their light, the earth sinks, while in the temple, a place of God's presence, the curtain that protects the sanctuary is rent in two. Jesus' death is characterised explicitly as a cosmic and a liturgical event; in particular, it marks the beginning of a new form of worship, in a temple not built by men, because it is the very Body of Jesus who died and rose which gathers peoples together and unites them in the sacrament of his Body and his Blood.

## Filial relationship

At this moment of suffering Jesus' prayer, "Father into your hands I commit my spirit", is a loud cry of supreme and total entrustment to God. This prayer expresses the full awareness that he had not been abandoned. The initial invocation - "Father" - recalls his first declaration as a twelve-year-old boy. At that time he had stayed for three days in the Temple of Jerusalem, whose veil was now torn in two. And when his parents had told him of their anxiety, he had answered: "How is it that you sought me? Did you not know that I must be in my Father's house?" (*Lk* 2:49). From the beginning to the end, what fully determines Jesus' feelings, words and actions, is his

unique relationship with the Father. On the Cross he lives
to the full, in love, this filial relationship he has with God
which gives life to his prayer.

## Jesus entrusts himself to God

The words spoken by Jesus after his invocation, "Father",
borrow a sentence from Psalm 31[30]: "into your hand
I commit my spirit" (*Ps* 31[30]:6). Yet these words are
not a mere citation but rather express a firm decision:
Jesus "delivers" himself to the Father in an act of total
abandonment. These words are a prayer of "entrustment":
total trust in God's love. Jesus' prayer as he faces death is
dramatic as it is for every human being but, at the same
time, it is imbued with that deep calmness that is born from
trust in the Father and from the desire to commend oneself
totally to him. In Gethsemane, when he had begun his final
struggle and his most intense prayer and was about to be
"delivered into the hands of men" (*Lk* 9:44), his sweat
had become "like great drops of blood falling down upon
the ground" (*Lk* 22:44). Nevertheless his heart was fully
obedient to the Father's will, and because of this "an angel
from heaven" came to strengthen him (cf. *Lk* 22:42-43).
Now, in his last moments, Jesus turns to the Father, telling
him into whose hands he really commits his whole life.
Before starting out on his journey towards Jerusalem, Jesus
had insisted to his disciples: "Let these words sink into your
ears; for the Son of man is to be delivered into the hands of

men" (*Lk* 9:44). Now that life is about to depart from him, he seals his last decision in prayer: Jesus let himself be delivered "into the hands of men", but it is into the hands of the Father that he places his spirit; thus - as the Evangelist John affirms - all was finished, the supreme act of love was carried to the end, to the limit and beyond the limit.

## Pray as Christ did

The words of Jesus on the Cross at the last moments of his earthly life offer us demanding instructions for our prayers, but they also open us to serene trust and firm hope. Jesus, who asks the Father to forgive those who are crucifying him, invites us to take the difficult step of also praying for those who wrong us, who have injured us, ever able to forgive, so that God's light may illuminate their hearts; and he invites us to live in our prayers the same attitude of mercy and love with which God treats us; "forgive us our trespasses and forgive those who trespass against us", we say every day in the Lord's Prayer. At the same time, Jesus, who at the supreme moment of death entrusts himself totally to the hands of God the Father, communicates to us the certainty that, however harsh the trial, however difficult the problems, however acute the suffering may be, we shall never fall from God's hands, those hands that created us, that sustain us and that accompany us on our way through life, because they are guided by an infinite and faithful love. Many thanks.

# Ash Wednesday

In this Catechesis, I would like to reflect briefly upon the season of Lent which begins today with the Ash Wednesday Liturgy. It is a 40-day journey that will bring us to the Easter Triduum - the memorial of the Lord's Passion, death and Resurrection, the heart of the mystery of our salvation. In the first centuries of the Church's life this was the time when those who had heard and received the proclamation of Christ set out, step by step, on their journey of faith and conversion in order to receive the sacrament of Baptism. For the catechumens - namely, those who wished to become Christian and to be incorporated into Christ and into the Church - it was a matter of drawing closer to the living God and an initiation to faith which was to take place gradually, through inner transformation.

## A time of repentance

Subsequently, penitents and then all the faithful were also asked to make this journey of spiritual renewal and increasingly to conform their lives to Christ's. The participation of the whole community in the various stages of the Lenten journey emphasises an important dimension of Christian spirituality: Christ's death and Resurrection does not bring the redemption of a few but of all. For this reason everyone, both those who were making a journey of faith as catechumens to receive Baptism and those who had drifted away from God and from the community of faith and were seeking reconciliation, as well as those who were living their faith in full communion with the Church, knew that the season which precedes Easter is a time of *metanoia*, that is, of a change of heart, of repentance; it is the season that identifies our human life and the whole of history as a process of conversion that starts now in order to encounter the Lord at the end of time.

## The symbolism of *Quadragesima*

Using an expression that has become characteristic in the liturgy, the Church calls the season we have entered today "*Quadragesima*", namely, a 40-day period, and, with a clear reference to Sacred Scripture, in this way introduces us into a precise spiritual context. In fact, 40 is the symbolic number with which both the Old and the New Testaments represent the salient moments in the experience of faith of the People of God. It is a number that stands for the time of waiting, of purification, of the return to the Lord, of the knowledge that God keeps his promises. This number does not represent an exact chronological period, marked by the sum of its days. Rather, it suggests patient perseverance, a long trial, a sufficient length of time in which to perceive God's works, a time within which one must resolve to assume one's responsibilities with no further postponement. It is the time for mature decisions.

## The number 40 in the Old and New Testaments

The number 40 first appears in the story of Noah. Because of the flood this righteous man spends 40 days and 40 nights in the Ark, with his family and with the animals that God had told him to take with him. And he waits another 40 days, after the flood, before touching dry land, saved from destruction (cf. *Gn* 7:4,12; 8:6). Then, the next stage: Moses remains in the Lord's presence on Mount Sinai for 40 days and 40 nights to receive the Law. He fasts throughout this period (cf. *Ex* 24:18). The journey of the Jewish people from Egypt to the Promised Land lasts for 40 years, an appropriate span of time to experience God's faithfulness. "You shall remember all the way which the Lord your God has led you these forty years in the wilderness … your clothing did not wear out upon you, and your foot did not swell, these forty years", Moses says in Deuteronomy at the end of the 40 years' migration (8:2, 4). The years of peace that Israel enjoys under the Judges are 40 (cf. 3:11, 30); but once this time has passed, forgetfulness of God's gifts and the return to sin creep in. The Prophet Elijah takes 40 days to reach Mount Horeb, the mountain where he encounters God (cf. *1 K* 19:8). For 40 days the inhabitants of Ninevah do penance in order to obtain God's forgiveness (cf. *Jon* 3:4). Forty is also the number of years of the reigns of Saul (cf. *Ac* 13:21), of David (cf. *2 S* 5:4-5) and of Solomon (cf. *1 K* 11:42), the first three kings of Israel. The Psalms also reflect on the biblical significance of the 40 years; for example, Psalm 95[94], a passage of which we have just heard: "O that today you would hearken to his voice! Harden not your hearts, as at Meribah, as on the day at Massah in the wilderness, when your fathers tested me, and put me to the proof, though they had seen my work. For forty years I loathed that generation and said, 'They are a people who err in heart, and they do not regard my ways'" (vv. 7c-10).

In the New Testament, before beginning his public ministry, Jesus withdraws into the wilderness for 40 days, neither eating nor drinking (cf. *Mt* 4:2); his nourishment is the word of God, which he uses as a weapon to triumph over the devil. Jesus' temptations recall those that the Jewish people faced in the desert, but which they were unable to overcome. It is for 40 days that the Risen Jesus instructs his disciples before ascending into Heaven and sending the Holy Spirit (cf. *Ac* 1:3).

## Israel's 40 years in the desert

This recurring number of 40 describes a spiritual context which is still timely and applicable, and the Church, precisely by means of the days of the Lenten season, wishes to preserve their enduring value and show us their effectiveness. The purpose of the Christian liturgy of Lent is to encourage a journey of spiritual renewal in the light

of this long biblical experience and, especially, to learn to
imitate Jesus, who by spending 40 days in the wilderness
taught how to overcome temptation with the word of
God. The 40 years that Israel spent wandering through
the wilderness reveal ambivalent attitudes and situations.
On the one hand they are the season of the first love with
God and between God and his people, when he speaks to
their hearts, continuously pointing out to them the path to
follow. God had, as it were, made his dwelling place in
Israel's midst: he went before his people in a cloud or in
a pillar of fire; he provided food for them every day by
bringing down manna from heaven and making water flow
from the rock. The years that Israel spent in the wilderness
can thus be seen as the time of God's predilection, the
time when the People adhered to him: a time of first love.
On the other hand, the Bible also shows another image
of Israel's wanderings in the wilderness: the time of the
greatest temptations and dangers too, when Israel mutters
against its God and, feeling the need to worship a God
who is closer and more tangible, would like to return to
paganism and build its own idols. It is also the time of
rebellion against the great and invisible God.

## Intimacy with God and temptation

In Jesus' earthly pilgrimage we are surprised to discover
this ambivalence, a time of special closeness to God - a time
of first love - and a time of temptation - the temptation to

return to paganism, but of course without any compromise with sin. After his Baptism of penance in the Jordan, when he takes upon himself the destiny of the Servant of God who renounces himself, lives for others and puts himself among sinners to take the sin of the world upon himself, Jesus goes into the wilderness and remains there for 40 days in profound union with the Father, thereby repeating Israel's history, with all those cadences of 40 days or years which I have mentioned. This dynamic is a constant in the earthly life of Jesus, who always seeks moments of solitude in order to pray to his Father and to remain in intimate communion, in intimate solitude with him, in an exclusive communion with him, and then to return to the people. However in this period of "wilderness" and of his special encounter with the Father, Jesus is exposed to danger and is assaulted by the temptation and seduction of the Evil One, who proposes a different messianic path to him, far from God's plan because it passes through power, success and domination rather than the total gift of himself on the Cross. This is the alternative: a messianism of power, of success, or a messianism of love, of the gift of self.

## The Church in the wilderness

This situation of ambivalence also describes the condition of the Church journeying through the "wilderness" of the world and of history. In this "desert" we believers certainly have the opportunity for a profound experience of God who strengthens the spirit, confirms faith, nourishes hope and awakens charity - an experience that enables us to share in Christ's victory over sin and death through his sacrifice of love on the Cross. However the "wilderness" is also a negative aspect of the reality that surrounds us: aridity, the poverty of words of life and of values, secularism and cultural materialism, which shut people into the worldly horizons of existence, removing them from all reference to transcendence. This is also the environment in which the sky above us is dark, because it is covered with the clouds of selfishness, misunderstanding and deceit. In spite of this, for the Church today the time spent in the wilderness may be turned into a time of grace, for we have the certainty that God can make the living water that quenches thirst and brings refreshment gush from even the hardest rock.

## Easter Resurrection

In these 40 days that will bring us to the Resurrection at Easter, we can find fresh courage for accepting with patience and faith every situation of difficulty, affliction and trial, in the knowledge that from the darkness the Lord will cause a new day to dawn. And if we are faithful to Jesus, following him on the Way of the Cross, the clear world of God, the world of light, truth and joy will be, as it were, restored to us. It will be the new dawn, created by God himself. A good Lenten journey to you all!

# On the Silence of Jesus

In a preceding series of Catecheses I have spoken of Jesus' prayer and I would not like to conclude this reflection without briefly considering the topic of Jesus' silence, so important in his relationship with God.

## Silence of the Cross

In the Post-Synodal Apostolic Exhortation *Verbum Domini*, I spoke of the role that silence plays in Jesus' life, especially on Golgotha: "Here we find ourselves before 'the word of the Cross' (cf. *1 Co* 1:18). The word is muted; it becomes mortal silence, for it has 'spoken' exhaustively, holding back nothing of what it had to tell us" (n. 12). Before this silence of the Cross, St Maximus the Confessor puts this phrase on the lips of the Mother of God: "Wordless is the Word of the Father, who made every creature which speaks, lifeless are the eyes of the one at whose word and whose nod all living things move!" (*Life of Mary,* n. 89: *Testi mariani del primo millennio*, 2, Rome, 1989, p. 253).

## The silence of God

The Cross of Christ does not only demonstrate Jesus' silence as his last word to the Father but reveals that God also *speaks* through *silence*: "The silence of God, the experience of the distance of the almighty Father, is a decisive stage in the earthly journey of the Son of God, the Incarnate Word. Hanging from the wood of the Cross, he lamented the suffering caused by that silence: 'My God, my God, why have you forsaken me?' (*Mk* 15:34; *Mt* 27:46). Advancing in obedience to his very last breath, in the obscurity of death, Jesus called upon the Father. He commended himself to him at the moment of passage, through death, to eternal life: 'Father, into your hands I commend my spirit' (*Lk* 23:46)" (Post-Synodal Apostolic Exhortation *Verbum Domini*, n. 21). Jesus' experience on the Cross profoundly reveals the situation of the person praying and the culmination of his prayer: having heard and recognised the word of God, we must also come to terms with the silence of God, an important expression of the same divine Word.

## Inner silence

The dynamic of words and silence which marks Jesus' prayer throughout his earthly existence, especially on the Cross, also touches our own prayer life in two directions. The first is the one that concerns the acceptance of the word of God. Inward and outward silence are necessary if we are to be able to hear this word. And in our time this point is particularly difficult for us. In fact, ours is an era that does not encourage recollection; indeed, one sometimes gets the impression that people are frightened of being cut off, even for an instant, from the torrent of words and images that mark and fill the day. It was for this reason that in the above mentioned Exhortation *Verbum Domini* I recalled our need to learn the value of silence: "Rediscovering the centrality of God's word in the life of the Church also means rediscovering a sense of recollection and inner repose. The great patristic tradition teaches us that the mysteries of Christ all involve silence. Only in silence can the word of God find a home in us, as it did in Mary, woman of the word and, inseparably, woman of silence" (n. 66).

## Silence in prayer

This principle - that without silence one does not hear, does not listen, does not receive a word - applies especially to personal prayer as well as to our liturgies: to facilitate authentic listening, they must also be rich in moments of silence and of non-verbal reception. St Augustine's observation is still valid: *Verbo crescente, verba deficiunt* - "when the word of God increases, the words of men fail" (cf. *Sermo* 288, 5: PL 38, 1307; *Sermo* 120, 2: PL 38, 677). The Gospels often present Jesus, especially at times of crucial decisions, withdrawing to lonely places, away from the crowds and even from the disciples in order to pray in silence and to live his filial relationship with God. Silence can carve out an inner space in our very depths to enable God to dwell there, so that his word will remain within us and so that love for him will take root in our minds and hearts and inspire our life. Hence the first direction: relearning silence, openness to listening, which opens us to the other, to the word of God.

## God knows what we need

However, there is also a second important connection between silence and prayer. Indeed it is not only our silence that disposes us to listen to the word of God. In our prayers we often find we are confronted by God's silence; we feel, as it were, let down: it seems to us that God neither listens nor responds. Yet God's silence, as happened to Jesus, does not indicate his absence. Christians know well that the Lord is present and listens, even in the darkness of pain, rejection and loneliness. Jesus reassures his disciples and each one of us that God is well acquainted with our needs at every moment of our life. He teaches the disciples: "In praying do not heap up empty phrases as the Gentiles do; for they think that they will be heard for their many words. Do not be like them, for your Father knows what you need before you ask him" (*Mt* 6:7-8): an attentive, silent and open heart is more important than many words.

## A deeper relationship with God

God knows us in our inmost depths, better than we ourselves, and loves us; and knowing this must suffice. In the Bible Job's experience is particularly significant in this regard. In a short time this man lost everything: relatives, possessions, friends and health. It truly seems that God's attitude to him was one of abandonment, of total silence. Yet in his relationship with God, Job speaks to God, cries out to God; in his prayers, in spite of all, he keeps his faith intact, and in the end, discovers the value of his experience and of God's silence. And thus he can finally conclude, addressing the Creator: "I had heard of you by the hearing of the ear, but now my eye sees you" (*Jb* 42:5): almost all of us know God only through hearsay and the more open we are to his silence and to our own silence, the more we truly begin to know him. This total trust that opens us to the profound encounter with God is developed in silence. St Francis Xavier prayed to the Lord saying: I do not love you because you can give me paradise or condemn me to hell, but because you are my God. I love you because You are You.

### Jesus teaches by example

As we reach the end of the reflections on Jesus' prayer, certain teachings of the *Catechism of the Catholic Church* spring to mind: "The drama of prayer is fully revealed to us in the Word who became flesh and dwells among us. To seek to understand his prayer through what his witnesses proclaim to us in the Gospel is to approach the holy Lord Jesus as Moses approached the burning bush: first to contemplate him in prayer, then to hear how he teaches us to pray, in order to know how he hears our prayer" (n. 2598). So, how does Jesus teach us to pray? We find a clear answer in the *Compendium of the Catechism of the Catholic Church*: "Jesus teaches us to pray not only with the Our Father" - certainly the high point of his instruction on how to pray - "but also when he prays. In this way he teaches us, in addition to the content, the dispositions necessary for every true prayer: purity of heart that seeks the Kingdom and forgives enemies, bold and filial faith that goes beyond what we feel and understand, and watchfulness that protects the disciple from temptation" (n. 544).

## Intimacy with God through prayer

In going through the Gospels we have seen that concerning our prayers the Lord is conversation partner, friend, witness and teacher. The newness of our dialogue with God is revealed in Jesus: the filial prayer that the Father expects of his children. And we learn from Jesus that constant prayer helps us to interpret our life, make our decisions, recognise and accept our vocation, discover the talents that God has given us and do his will daily, the only way to fulfil our life.

Jesus' prayer points out to us, all too often concerned as we are with operational efficacy and the practical results we achieve, that we need to pause, to experience moments of intimacy with God, "detaching ourselves" from the everyday commotion in order to listen, to go to the "root" that sustains and nourishes life. One of the most beautiful moments of Jesus' prayer is precisely when - in order to deal with the illnesses, hardships and limitations of those who are conversing with him - he turns to the Father in prayer and thereby teaches those around him where to seek the source of hope and salvation.

## God answers our prayers

I have already recalled as a moving example Jesus' prayer at the tomb of Lazarus. The Evangelist John recounts: "So they took away the stone. And Jesus lifted up his eyes and said, 'Father, I thank you that you have heard me. I knew that you hear me always, but I have said this on account of the people standing by, that they may believe that you sent me'. When he had said this, he cried with a loud voice, 'Lazarus, come out'" (*Jn* 11:41-43). However, Jesus reaches the most profound depths in prayer to the Father at the moment of his Passion and his death when he says the extreme "yes" to God's plan and shows how the human will finds its fulfilment precisely in full adherence to the divine will rather than in opposition to it. In Jesus' prayer, in his cry to the Father on the Cross, are summed up "all the troubles, for all time, of humanity enslaved by sin and death, all the petitions and intercessions of salvation history.... Here the Father accepts them and, beyond all hope, answers them by raising his Son. Thus is fulfilled and brought to completion the drama of prayer in the economy of creation and salvation" (*Catechism of the Catholic Church* n. 2606).

Let us trustingly ask the Lord to grant that we live the journey of our filial prayer learning daily from the Only-Begotten Son, who became man for our sake, what should be our way of addressing God. St Paul's words on Christian life in general also apply to our prayers: "I am sure that neither death, nor life, nor angels, nor principalities, nor things present, nor things to come, nor powers, nor height, nor depth, nor anything else in all creation, will be able to separate us from the love of God in Christ Jesus our Lord" (*Rm* 8:38-39).

# Sources

*Prayer Throughout the Life of Jesus*: General Audience, 30 November 2011, Paul VI Audience Hall.

*The Cry of Exultation*: General Audience, 7 December 2011, Paul VI Audience Hall

*The Prayer of Jesus Linked to His Miraculous Healing Action*: General Audience, 14 December 2011, Paul VI Audience Hall.

*Prayer and the Holy Family of Nazareth*: General Audience, 28 December 2011, Paul VI Audience Hall.

*Jesus' Prayer at the Last Supper*: General Audience, 11 January 2012, Paul VI Audience Hall.

*On the Priestly Prayer of Jesus*: General Audience, 25 January 2012, Paul VI Audience Hall.

*Jesus' Prayer at Gethsemane*: General Audience, 1 February 2012, Paul VI Audience Hall.

*Jesus' Prayer in the Face of Death* (*Matthew and Mark*): General Audience, 8 February 2012, Paul VI Audience Hall.

*On the Last Three "Words" of Jesus Dying on the Cross (Luke)*: General Audience, 15 February 2012, Paul VI Audience Hall.

*Ash Wednesday*: General Audience, 22 February 2012, Paul VI Audience Hall

*On the Silence of Jesus*: General Audience, 7 March 2012, Saint Peter's Square.